Soulful Parenting

Heather Lupick

DISCERN
PRODUCTS

Published by:
Discern Products
724 Parkdale Ave.
Ottawa, ON K1Y 1J6
info@discernproducts.com
www.discernproducts.com

ISBN 978-1-988422-22-0

Cover design by Heather Lupick
Photos by Kryna Pohl, Marilyn Savage and Heather Lupick

Printed by Kindle Direct Publishing

Contents

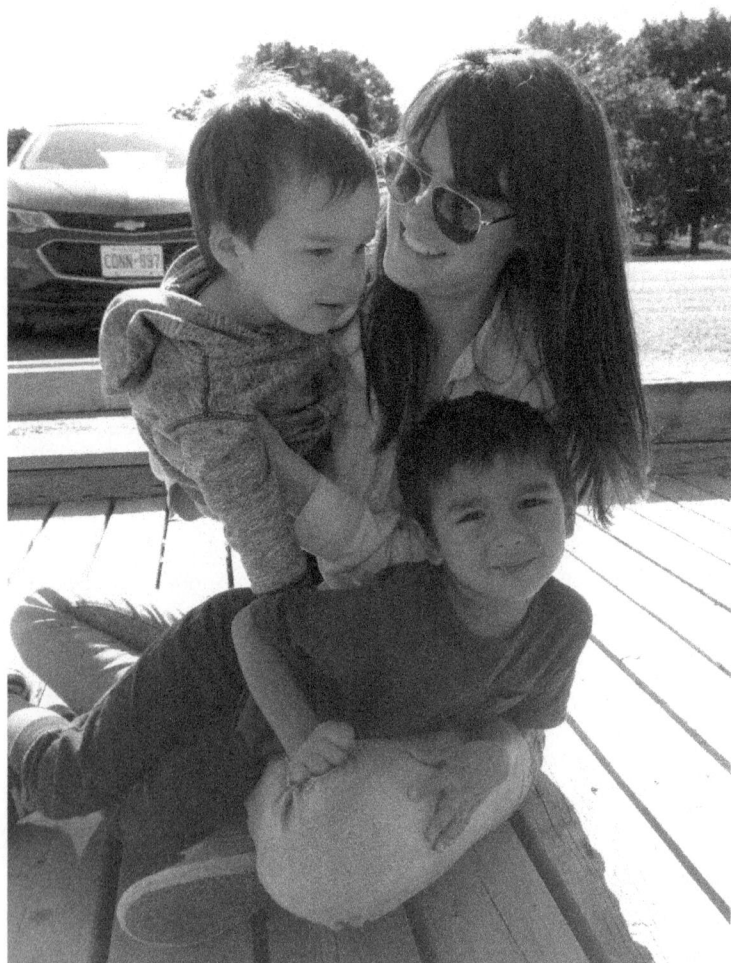

Week 1

Setting the foundation for the soulful parenting journey

As parents we have embarked on a journey marked with both joys and challenges, full of delightful moments of love and painful moments of anger and tears. All of what we experience is a part of the stark reality of our human lives as parents. Sometimes the day in and day out routine can become daunting in and of itself and our souls long for something more. There is a calling inside us yearning for a rich place of connection with our children and with God.

In the soulful parenting journey, everyday moments can become opportunities for connection, for joy, for reflection, for noticing the sacred. They become life giving invitations to see and to hear God and to guide our children to potentially see him too. When our hearts become softened to the possibilities that moments which once may have seemed pointlessly challenging become moments of beauty and growth, then we begin to come alive.

We each enter this parenting journey with our own unique personalities and our own unique stories. These effect the ways we parent and the aspects which are most challenging and difficult for us. The traumatic and wounding moments we had in our own childhoods have been partially instrumental in effecting the way in which we respond to our children, to ourselves, and to God when those wounds are touched. Some of these places need to be healed and restored; our hearts need to hear new messages and our perspectives need to shift so that we are able to lead our children into healthy places that we have not known.

Along the way we will journey together into the depths of our hearts. Where are we able to meet ourselves, our children and God with the depths of our truth? As we walk the daily moments of our lives we will begin to implement little practices here and there that will draw our awareness to the sacred beauty of God in the midst of our relationship with our children. This is the soulful journey, living honestly before God, ourselves and our children and beginning to shift our inner eyes to notice the divine in the mundane.

Journaling Questions:
(bring all these before God in a prayerful heart space)

- What do I long for in my relationship with my children?

- What messages does my heart want my children to hear?

- What areas of my relationship with my children do I feel are life giving?

- What areas of my relationship with my children do I feel burdened by?

- What are my fears in regards to my children or my relationship with them?

- In what circumstances do I feel most aware of past wounding?

Applications:

- Take a verse and depict it in painting with your children (suggestion: Psalm 23).

- Light a sweet-smelling candle together and remind your child of the verse that talks of our lives as a sweet fragrance to God (reference: 2 Corinthians 2:15).

- Bake together and talk about God as our nourishment our bread of life (reference: John 6:35).

- When you wash the dishes together this week, take a moment not only to feel the warm clean water flowing over your hands feeling gratitude rising up in your heart, but also a moment to talk about how God is the living water who washes us clean and who quenches our thirst (reference: John 4:14).

Setting the foundation

SOULFUL PARENTING

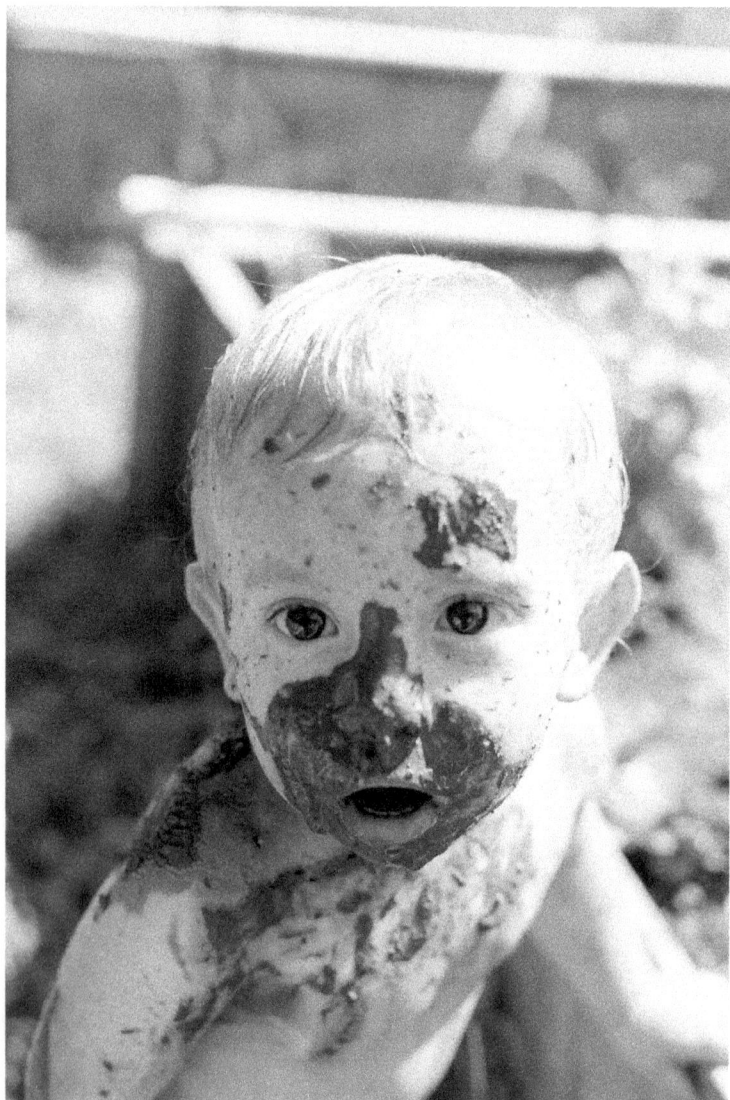

Week 2

Growing through gratitude: seeing God in all the beautiful little things

Crunching through the cold snow with bundled children, listening to their squeaky boots as they toddle beside...watching our breath heave into the air, life made visible as warmth hits cold...holding small-mittened hands... feeling soft snowflakes fluttering down onto our eager exploring tongues...

So many joyful discoveries to appreciate. Let your mind begin to see each precious moment and give thanks. Throughout the day there are so many moments to notice, to be aware of, to observe and to appreciate that often remain unseen. It is easy to allow our minds to be preoccupied with many things and not invite ourselves to embrace the sacred space we need in order to appreciate. Gratitude is paramount to our lives as human beings and in our particular lives as parents. God calls us and invites us to worship, praise and adore him. Over and over he beckons to us to truly see him in his glory and to marvel. Thankfulness and gratitude are practices that expand our hearts to love, goodness, joy and inclusiveness. They are one such way for our souls to receive life giving nutrients even by way of us offering up the sacrifice. This opens our hearts to connect ever more deeply with the precious gifts who are our children...

Hearing the screeches of frustrated children as icy snow hits their bare wrists, tears of relief glistening in their trusting eyes as you come to their rescue once again...swooping them up as they tumble into the fluffy drifts watching as snow sticks to their gorgeous eyelashes...seeing the childlike compassion of the little one as he bends to touch the fallen sibling "happened? Ok?"... seeing God's abundant grace in the extended forgiveness of a wronged sibling – quick to jump back into play after a moment of fiery anger.

Let's embrace gratitude of the bittersweet rays of sun after the rain. So often we are consumed by the emotions of the precipitating event. Our parent hearts are constantly being jolted into awareness of the need for intervention or refereeing. We forget to settle the little adrenaline rush and notice the rays of sun shining through those cloudy moments. These moments are just as impactful on our children's growing character and spirit as are the purely joyful ones. These moments are also just as or even more impactful on us if we consciously choose to accept them as they are and see them for the totality of their whole from beginning to end. Let's begin to intentionally look for the ways of redemption in each moment – allowing our hearts to experience gratitude and extending thanks to the Lord for his working grace in our lives and the lives of our children. Speak your gratitude aloud as a beacon for your children to hear and follow.

What of the stormy moments that don't seem to conclude in beauty? What of the tantruming child, the slamming door, the spilled cheerios, the constant bickering, the sensory overload meltdowns, the bullying at school, the doctor's frightening news, the difficult attitude, the drugs, the eating disorders or the teen relationships... Do our heart's still hold the capacity for gratitude even in the moments when we are weeping? Are we able to see and acknowledge God in the midst of our gut-wrenching moments of pain? Do we trust him enough to bring our full laments before him where in the end we can still say (maybe through gritted teeth :) "Yet I will still praise you, for you are faithful, you are with me!"

Let's grab a hold of RADICAL gratitude, the kind of gratitude that will rock us to our core!

Journaling Questions:

- Write down glimpses of beauty you are grateful for (each day this week).

- What do you find hard about gratitude?

- Do you find there are areas of your life with children that are hard to express thanks in? Express these as deeply as you need to.

- Are there areas you find more easy to be grateful in? Express these as elaborately as possible!

Applications:

- Ask each of your children to notice something beautiful and share.

- Try eating mindfully – savouring slowly each bite you take, include your children in this practice.

- Say something thoughtful and kind to each of your children and hold in your heart the look in their eyes.

- Hold your children close, smell their sweet smells, feel their soft hair and skin, listen to their quiet breath and heartbeat.

- Lay down on the ground outside and look at the clouds, treetops or the stars – wonder together about how awesome it all is.

SOULFUL PARENTING

Growing through gratitude

Week 3

Whispers in the challenges: transformational ground in triggers and conflict

As human beings our natural inclination is to avoid suffering. Suffering is a part of life that is completely undesirable. In body, mind and spirit we strive to achieve optimum and ideal states of being. We search for peace, comfort, joy and blessing and our brain screams "No!" when we experience physical, emotional or spiritual pain and discomfort. We don't want suffering for ourselves, or those that we love. We long to protect our children, and we long to protect our relationship from the natural strife and conflict that occurs between two intimately bonded people. Experiencing this conflict can raise up in us a number of conflicting emotions. These also may change depending on the nature of the challenges as well as the influence from the wounds of our own life being stroked and coming up to be heard and attended to. We might experience, fear, anger, frustration, sadness, guilt or shame. These emotions are messages for us about something going on under the surface. Rather than suppressing or ignoring, perhaps these emotions and these moments might serve as

15

transformative if we hold them with wonder asking the Holy Spirit to open our eyes.

Suffering is capable of producing profound inner growth if we choose to embrace its offerings. In the true embracing of the suffering we accept an invitation to a collective connection with every living being who has also embraced that sacred space. In the course of our lives as parents we will have micro and macro moments of conflict and pain associated with our interactions with our children. Each of these moments will have an impact on us and they will have an impact on our children. It is in these moments and as we look over the sum total of these moments where we have the choice to harden or soften our hearts. The choices we make will affect our relationship with our children, others, ourselves and God. Conversely these choices will also affect our children's relationship with us, others, themselves and God.

We all come into our role as parents wounded in some way or another - those of us who came from healthy families and those of us who experienced severe abuse or trauma. Our childhood in all its wondrous moments also contained moments of pain that made a mark on our hearts and imprinted messages on our souls. As we take these into our parenting relationship it impacts the way we relate to our children and the way we react to various situations. Suffering is often a very subjective and highly personal experience. What stirs up suffering in one person may not in another. It is important for us to live with the awareness of our wounds so that we are not being led blindly. Taking the effort, soul space and time to notice our reactions and patterns of relating is paramount to the healing and restoration of our hearts. Of great importance is forgiveness of those from the past who have inflicted some of the pain that causes our reactions. Without forgiving and repenting of our judgement, bitterness, or resentment towards that person we are much more likely to continue perpetuating the same patterns. As we release these things at the cross, we receive healing and restoration in our sensitive areas.

When we mindfully and intentionally engage with our children, with the awareness and hopefully healing of past wounds, through the work of the Holy Spirit, the conflict or situation loses much of its power to overwhelm us. Hence we will be passing on to our children more holistically healthy responses and models of behaviour.

So in the midst of our day to day interactions and conflicts how can we listen to God's voice speaking and gently leading us towards growth? As we feel the tension mounting in the room let's invite ourselves into a new pattern of taking an internal moment of space. In this moment can we ask ourselves: What are the needs of my child? What are my needs? What are the underlying emotions? What are some past wounds or messages that might be playing into either side of the interactions? Is there something the Holy Spirit is saying or inviting me to in this moment? These can be some of the most trying moments as parents when we enter into conflict with our children. This is challenging ground and takes considerable self control and diligence to respond in new ways to change old patterns of relating and to train ourselves to look for God in the middle of it.

Once the relationship has been reconciled and peace returns then is the time to talk your children through these similar steps. Instill in them the value of stopping for a internal moment of space to ask themselves similar questions you are asking yourself and to listen for the voice of God - his invitations, challenges and convictions. Perhaps you wish to create a code word that either of you could use to indicate you need to take that spacious moment. Perhaps you wish to adopt a designated spot in your house where you sit either to listen to the Holy Spirit or to negotiate peace together, you and your child.

It is also deeply important for children to learn the respect of boundaries. Without boundaries the world becomes an unsafe reality for both your child and for those effected by your children. The ramifications of boundary-less living stretches into adulthood and can affect our adult integration into society. It is of vital importance that we all internalize the respect and dignity integral to keeping boundaries. Boundaries and the crossing of boundaries effects all of us in every relationship we have. It also effects the way we interact within both our social networks and also importantly our obedience to the law. If children are raised to believe they are entitled to act, behave and treat people as they wish their consciences will not be developed such that they will live in conformity to the law. Of course even more importantly we want them to understand the intrinsic value of respecting boundaries not just to conform for the sake of avoiding consequence, but because of the honour this shows to God. Therefore if there is a conflict that arises and you have considered your child's needs and feelings but know that you need to place this boundary than you as their authority need to do so for their own good.

These practices will of course also effect sibling relationships, peer relationships and relationships with other adults. Moments of conflict or suffering are sacred invitations into something deeper, as you are submerged you arise with an enlarged capacity for compassion, kindness, and wisdom.

Journaling Questions:

- What is your natural response to challenges and conflict within your family?

- Do you notice a pattern of those situations or moments that tend to stroke a sensitive spot in you? Pray that God would help you explore those areas more deeply so you can experience healing and restoration.

- Give an example of a time when you've felt the convicting prodding of the Holy Spirit in the midst of conflict with your children that has invited you to transformation.

Applications:

- Notice the patterns of where conflict arises in your family and the emotional response in you.

- Pray God would open your ears and then listen in the midst of each conflict for where God is asking you to grow.

- Choose healthy moments where you are able to guide your children through this same process to hear God and discern how he is asking them to grow.

- Chose and set up your sacred space, your peace table or your code word.

SOULFUL PARENTING

Whispers in the challenges

SOULFUL PARENTING

Week 4

The sacred ground of tears: space for your child's emotions, and space for your own

To be witness to the raw vulnerability of tears is a beautiful invitation into someone's soul. Tears are a wordless expression of a person's inner turmoil, angst, sorrow, lament, grief, frustration or even joy. They are the overflow and external illustration of the internal places of a person's heart. Overtime we have learned to control our tears and often suppress them for the sake of conforming to the cultural norms in which we find ourselves. The intense, unvarnished nature of tears calls out for us to respond, to connect, to perceive, to merge with. In general the depth of these connections are difficult. Many of us as children were told to hide our tears, sometimes being shamed for them whether in subtle or obvious ways. This has created within us an unnatural aversion, angst or even fear towards tears as they represent something almost taboo. We sense the invitation to places that are unfamiliar to us. What will be expected of us when we get there? Is it safe? What does it feel like to enter the unguarded spaces?

Children in their innocence and naivety have yet to learn or desire to guard themselves particularly with those to whom they are attached and feel safe. Their natural inclination is to share their tears, to cry and express with those who love them. That is the true desire inside all of us. If we can learn to embrace our own tears, we can give that gift of acceptance to our children too. This gift has a massive positive impact on their emotional, physical and spiritual health. Through our empathy, acceptance and love we as parents begin to show children God's tender heart towards them.

Though we may not want to admit it to ourselves the intensity and passion that comes with tears and the frequency of them can be overwhelming for us as parents. The request to be heard, and the volume that often accompanies these requests can feel intrusive, demanding, and inconvenient. The sacrifice to open our hearts up to receive our children's depths is often underestimated. This sacrifice is also invaluable, it's a treasure we have to offer to our children. If we can begin to both allow ourselves to shift our perspective and see the beautiful and sacred invitation they are offering AND to have a place where we ourselves are safely heard, the sacrifice may begin to feel more like an honour than a burden.

When we experience situations in our lives that are stressful or painful whether big or small our body stores these emotional memories as cortisol which needs to be released for the health of our body, mind and soul. Tears, raging, shaking, trembling, sweating and yawning are all physical ways in which cortisol is released. Manifestations and release of distress in various ways results in cortisol decrease. (https://www.ncbi.nlm.nih.gov/pmc/articles/PMC403556 8/). When this release becomes healing for us and for children is when we have an empathetic presence to hold us tenderly and to hear us. As adults we can provide that empathetic presence to ourselves, and hear the still voice and presence of God within us embracing us with his perfect empathy speaking to us in loving and accepting ways as we cry. Children do not have the capacity to be that presence for themselves; we as their parents become that inner voice for them that they adopt over time. We also teach them to hear God's voice so that he becomes that one they lean on. This is often why even as adults we can speak to ourselves quite harshly because we have adopted an inner voice that was not empathetic. As we intentionally choose a new voice and put this into practice this can change.

God who is described in both motherly and fatherly characteristics is our ultimate source of empathy. When we practice lamenting in his presence and allowing him to tenderly hold us with compassion we receive deep healing and restoration which has the capacity to meet our needs and to fill our cups enabling us to give back to our children in this same way. As we accept our children's tears and gift them with our empathy we are also given the opportunity to guide our children into God's nurturing arms so that they become dependent on him for their emotional and spiritual needs as they grow and mature.

As we have already begun last week exploring our reactions to conflict and the triggers of wounds from the past we may, this week, be ready to be more receptive to emotional expressions such as tears. As we continue along our journey let's give special attention to accepting and embracing tears as the gift that they are. Cultivate your relationship with God by sharing your tears with him. Connect with your children by gently and compassionately receiving their tears.

Journaling questions:

- Do you tend to be a person who holds tears inside or who cries often and easily?

- Do you feel comfortable with tears or do you have a conflicted relationship with them?

- What were the messages you received in regards to tears growing up?

- How do you respond to your child's tears?

- Where is God in the midst of tears, sorrow, lament?

Applications:

- This week pray that God would release your tears and spend some time journaling about your experience with this.

- Begin talking to your children about tears and creating a level of comfort with them and their expression of tearful feelings.

SOULFUL PARENTING

- Pray with your children and read scriptures together that show God as a compassionate presence for them who accepts them as they are.

The sacred ground of tears

Week 5

Wrestling with the anger: acceptance, redirection, glimpsing God's justice

Anger is a hot and difficult emotion for many of us in this culture. It is intense, fiery and passionate. Anger can be a hot surging feeling that is sometimes experienced as uncontrollable. Some of us have more of a tendency towards experiencing anger than others and have become accustomed to its quick and furious release throughout our bodies. Others of us feel overwhelmed by anger and avoid it at all costs. It can be a fearful experience to be overcome by such strong sensations with no idea what to do with them. As it courses through our veins everything inside us screams for release. It is usually much more highly enjoyable to stay in a peaceful state of calm, but it is not possible to completely avoid anger. Anger has its place in human reality and existence.

Just as we find anger difficult, our children also struggle with this emotion. As young toddlers they have yet to fully integrate the capacity for impulse control nor do they realize, until we guide them, that anger may not be immediately acted upon in whatever way their bodies desire. It can be very difficult for us to witness our children's anger and their often accompanying aggressive acts towards us, others or themselves. It can often stroke places within us that enliven our own angry responses and reactions. As we grow and learn to give anger its place of acceptance we are able to empathize with our children in their anger and separate our own internal responses from those which they are experiencing.

Children, just as we, need to learn that anger is not the enemy. It is not something to suppress, or disdain. Anger is simply another of our body's emotions. It is an emotion we often feel as a response to something that is not right. In its righteous form it is a response to injustice. Our hearts, bodies and souls cry out to bring justice into gut wrenching situations we are either immersed in or witness to. The deep places of our souls long for all things to be made right, redeemed, restored, and put into perfect order. Anger is that part of us that hopes to rail and rage against these wrongs to make them right again. Of course just as all emotions can come from selfish motivations so can anger. It is our task as we walk this journey to gently pull apart the false from the true and react accordingly. Next time you feel anger, stop and take a moment (hard but important to do) and ask yourself where is this coming from? What is the crux of the injustice I'm recognizing and reacting to? Help your children to do this too. Anger is an invitation to us to enter into the dance of justice and mercy.

Those of us who are more carried along and guided by emotions rather than more logical thought processes may find this a harder aspect to wrestle. Our amygdale, which is the emotional memory centre of our brain, loves to override our cortex, the logical thoughtful centre of our brain. But wrestle we must if we desire to bring anger under control and to allow its voice of justice to be heard. The majority of this wrestle will happen most fruitfully through prayer. The Holy Spirit will guide each of us into the places we need to go for healing in order to release these unproductive angry responses. This will be a beautiful example to our children and will do them much good to have this modelled to them throughout their lives. Anger is neither to be liberally freed nor coercively chained. If we can learn practices and pass these along to our children the invitations of anger will be able to take their rightful and honoured place in the lives of our families. We want anger to produce restoration not destruction. It certainly has the capacity for either.

Practices surrounding anger:

- Take a moment to uncover the underlying values or principles being prodded by the current circumstance.

- Do some deep breathing (breathe in for 8 and out for 4).

- Remind yourself there is no rule saying you must respond immediately (unless someone is in danger). Tell your child you need time before responding.

- When you feel ready give appropriate voice to your feelings. Speak to the injustice, the unmet need or expectation. Avoid attacking or putting others on defense.

- If there is time for either you or your child, engage in a physical activity such as running, walking, dancing, yoga, your favorite exercise program. This will help release the excess adrenaline and release endorphins into your system. Try not to use this a distraction or suppression, but use it as a method of releasing and controlling – and still provide voice to the underlying feelings when you are ready.

- If you or your child are struggling with chronic anger it may be time to explore the reasons behind this. This could be done through talk, prayer, inner healing ministry, play, art, or music amongst other ideas you may have.

Journaling questions:

- What were the messages you received as a child regarding anger?

- What does anger stir up inside you?

- What do you do when you are feeling angry?

- What messages intentional or not do you give to your children regarding anger?

- Can you think of a time when anger was used positively to spur you on to needed action or justice?

- Describe anger as it relates to God and his character.

Applications:

- Look up these verses about anger: James 1:19-20, Ephesians 4:26-27, Ecclesiastes 7:9, Psalm 7:11, Zechariah 8:2.

- Take some space to journal and release some anger to God in prayer then sit quietly to listen for his response. Allow yourself to feel the safety of his acceptance of you.

- Invite your children to talk to you about their anger. Discuss how it feels (my son describes it as a fiery dragon in his heart. He says that sometimes even when he tries to be kind the rude fire still comes out.) Give them guidance on what they can appropriately do with their anger.

- Provide materials (paper, magazines, paint, glue, scissors, stickers) for your child and artistically depict anger. Pray together that God would turn your anger into something good and just.

SOULFUL PARENTING

Wrestling with the anger

SOULFUL PARENTING

Week 6

Beauty of connection: deep ways of connecting with your child and with God

It is our deep desire as human beings to connect. We are created to long for connection. It is not good for us to be alone. Some of us tolerate and enjoy time alone more than others, but all of us need other bonds as a crucial aspect of being human and alive. Sometimes when we have been deeply wounded our desire for connection is skewed in various ways. Sometimes our fear holds us back from attempting to connect or permitting connection. Other times we become overly dependent and enmeshed in unhealthy relationships with others. This can also be true with the way that we interact with our children. Children need connection, they need a healthy God given connection – the kind he designed from the very beginning to be natural and nurturing between parents and children. Important scientific studies have been done on attachment, and the importance of secure attachment between parents and children. This bond is a significant precursor to psychological health all the way into adulthood. The early years are a vital period of time for brain development. What happens in these years is very impactful into the future. Fortunately, through brain studies we are learning about the plasticity of our neurological make up. This means that our minds even as we age have the potential for transformation. It is never too late. But how wonderful it can be if we start these healthy patterns of connection from a young age with our own children.

God as trinity is a look at a perfect consummated and unified love relationship. Making us in his own image he has planted within us that same desire that he has to connect. His heart is satisfied and fully nurtured through the loving bond he has within his own Holy self. Out of this fierce and all consuming love flows the love that embraces all of his creation. All creatures, not only human are swept up into this most passionate of loves. All goodness swirls and surrounds and fills through this love. As parents we can look to this love as an example to us of the love and connection we can have with our children. Through our connection our children's need for love will be met as well as showing them the connection they could have with God. This consistent connection we provide them can then continue internally and externally, with other relationships, even when we begin the process of differentiation as our children age. Connection with our children can be nurtured in many ways, all of which share a common denominator – our presence.

- In week 4 we explored the sacred ground of tears. Listening to tears and being present in these difficult and complex emotions will bring a profound sense of connection. To share with one another in our vulnerability and to be held in safety creates bonds that are strong and deep. It takes courage to open out hearts, to risk the pain of the severing of the very connection we are opening to. Despite this or perhaps even because of the risk unless we choose to do so we lose out on the very rich experiences of human existence. Listen to and accept as many tears as you have the capacity for. Gather a greater capacity by having your own tears heard in an appropriate relationship. Compassionate connection breeds the capacity for more compassionate connection.

- Create an atmosphere where you provide and engage in "spacious play" with your children. In this time you spend one on one time with your child where you practice mindfully attending to your child above and apart from all else. In a way this can become a meditative practice. You will give your child an incredible gift by learning to be completely present to them in ways that facilitate delightful interaction. In this time let your child choose what they would like to do with you and then attend to this with intentionality. Put away your phone, your computer and all other distractions. If unwanted thoughts cross your mind gently put them aside to deal with later and direct your mind back to your child and the current activity. This done in a rhythmic manner can be highly instrumental in facilitating deep bonding.

- Games that encourage laughter are also an excellent way to connect. Just as tears release more traumatic levels of stress, laughter releases lower levels of stress and fear. Laughter connects and bonds. It facilitates a space of acceptance through the freedom of silliness. Each child is an individual; what will bring laughter to one will not to another. Be sensitive to your child's personality, unique sense of humour and possible fears and stressors that have recently plagued them. If you can create laughter around one of these fears you will be accomplishing healing and restoration as well as connection. Be careful not to use embarrassment or shame to promote laughter, rather than facilitating connection this will ultimately create disconnection.

Through our own daily connection that we make with God we begin to demonstrate to our children ways that they also might connect with God. It's probably more common that our connections with God happen internally where many would not even realize it was occurring, but I might suggest that for the sake of our children we attempt to speak out loud the connections we are making. We could connect with God through verbal means such as: thanking him at various moments, sending out short prayers based on our concerns or our feelings, asking for help in guiding our actions or behaviour; through practicing his presence by pausing and intentionally turning our mind to his presence with us in that moment, by taking specific time to be silent and centered before him where we simply listen and feel him; by envisioning ourselves in visual locations with him at our sides; by meditating on him through music or art or nature; amongst others that you may think of.

Another very beautiful and important way of connecting with our children is through blessing them with words of encouragement, prayer and declarations. We see all throughout the Old Testament how this is a vital aspect of Hebrew culture. Parents bless their children. This is an excellent rhythm to create in a frequent ongoing capacity. It's also very impactful to speak a blessing over our children at large moments of transition such as graduations, becoming an adult or getting married. This helps to launch them from their roots onto their wings.

Journaling questions:

- Currently how connected do you feel to your child? To God?

- If you feel a certain level of disconnection what do you feel contributes to this?

- How comfortable and natural does it feel to engage in activities that promote intimate connection?

- As a child what level of connection did you feel to important adults or to God?

- Journal about anything uncomfortable or painful that comes up for you as you open your heart to give and receive connection.

Applications:

- Play some laughter inducing games with your children this week.

- Practice spacious play with your child for 10 minutes each day.

- Engage in a connective moment with God each day (this may be a nature walk, star or cloud gazing, worship singing, a hot bath with candles, painting scripture verses, using a tangible object in meditative prayer.)

- Ask God to show you in your mind's eye a sacred place where he can meet with you, then allow him to bond with you lovingly in that place (this might be imaginary or it might be material) (Ex: When I am afraid, or desperate, sorrowful or filled with longing I close my eyes and in my mind I go to this place I know called Meadow Creek. Here in the foothills of the Rockies with a creek, a cabin and some horses Jesus always meet me. We sit on the side of a hill in the still of the summer evening and I lay my head on his chest as he holds me in his arms. Often he speaks soothingly to me. Other times I have gone to this island in the middle of a lake and in the middle of the island is a grove of trees with a carpet of thick soft moss. The sunlight streams down through the trees and bathes the moss with scattered and iridescent light. I lay down in the moss with my eyes closed and I feel the light as God the Father wrapping me in a tender embrace – warm and all encompassing.)

• Guide your children to begin meeting God in these fulfilling ways too.

Beauty of connection

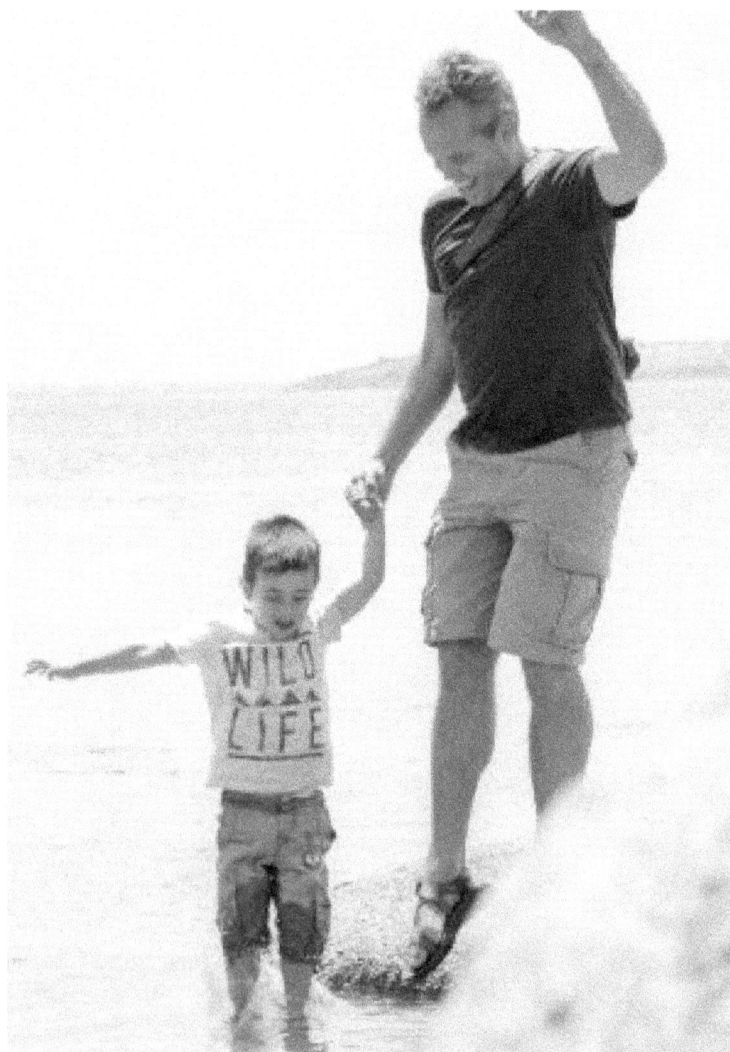

Week 7

Walking hand in hand: art of respect

It can be easy to go through the motions of daily life and not really take the time to hear each other or to immerse ourselves in the presence of one another. We rush about doing our own thing hardly giving attention to the people in front of us that matter. Let's take time this week to slow down, to stop, to listen, to linger...

Some of us are more likely to lean on the more authoritarian side of parenting, demanding respect for ourselves and hardly acknowledging the dignity and honour our children also deserve as human beings. Some of us on the other hand fall into permissive parenting where we don't create our own boundaries and our children end up with all the authority and the atmosphere is less than respectful from the other side. I believe God longs for us to sit somewhere in the middle, for there to be mutual respect and loving attention gifted in both directions. As our children see us maintaining our own boundaries of safety, speaking our wants and needs and directing them in moments where they don't have the capacity to make mature decisions they learn the importance of this for themselves over time. They both learn how to treat others and how to treat themselves with loving respect.

We want our children to have a voice, we don't want them to grow up fearful of speaking, expressing, challenging or passionately pursuing. We want them to know that we support and love them no matter what choices they make even if contrary to our own personal value system. This requires creating an environment that is safe and conducive to respectful discussion without fear of repercussion. Though our children are small, and less knowledgeable than we are they sometimes have incredible wisdom. God speaks to us through our children if we open our hearts to truly hear him and them. We also are instruments of wisdom and guidance to them which will be far more thoroughly imparted if surrounded in a case of respectful and loving embrace.

Despite the incredible difference in power, wisdom, knowledge, size and holiness between God and humans he treats us with the utmost dignity and respect. He sees us in our frailty and vulnerability and he gives us a place of honour. He listens to us and hears the cries of our hearts. He doesn't ignore, bark commands at us or expect immediate compliance. He gently holds our hand and walks with us along the difficult and challenging journey. This is a stark look at God and his care for us, and specifically his Hebrew people in Ezekiel 16 "When you were born, no one cut your umbilical cord. *No one took care of you:* you were not washed with water and purified, nor were you rubbed with salt and wrapped *for warmth.* No one felt sorry for you or had compassion on you or did anything to help you. Instead, *your parents abandoned you,* tossed you out into an open field. For on the day you were born, people looked upon you with deep contempt. Then I passed by and saw you squirming around in your blood. As you lay there in your own blood, I said to you, "Live!" Again, I insisted, "Live!" *And that's exactly what you did.* I helped you flourish like plants in the field. In time you grew, became a tall, beautiful young woman..."

Just as God has shown his exquisite love for us and carefully listened to our hearts and our words, let's return his love for us in the same way. Let's listen to our children, and let's listen to him. Let's teach our children to turn their eyes to him and listen too. When we all begin to compassionately listen to one another beauty begins to bloom. Our hearts are opened in a new and different way.

Journaling Questions:

- How do you tend to speak to your children?

- Are you in the rhythm of deeply listening to them or do you find yourself barely hearing them or only hearing on a superficial level?

- How do your children speak to and listen to you?

- Do you really listen to God?

Applications:

- Journal about a time when your child said something that had a profound impact on you.

- Practice true listening. When your child speaks take time to stop, make eye contact and physical connection, and hear her.

- Do a listening prayer exercise with your children. Help them begin listening for even a minute or two a day.

SOULFUL PARENTING

Walking hand in hand

Week 8

Ongoing practices: rhythms to maintain the ongoing practice of soulful parenting

As we journey along day by day with our children it is important to implement practices into the rhythms and routines of our days so that it all becomes a part of the fabric of our lives together as parents, children and God. Otherwise it is easy to become forgetful and to leave out the practices that connect us to one another and guide our children to notice God's presence in their lives. When we integrate and weave patterns together they become second nature to us and teach our brains to remember and naturally engage to the point that it would feel strange not to.

There can be many obstacles that stop us from integrating these practices into our lives. These can include: busyness, avoidance, fear, discomfort, selfishness, weariness, lack of energy, resistance or any number of others. The beauty and blessing of connecting deeply and soulfully with our children and God are worth the effort it may take to work past these obstacles and to live freely in these practices. Many of these obstacles come from deep seated wounds, messages or lies we believe within ourselves which need to be transformed and healed. When we do this sacred work our souls are opened up to embrace the soulful practices of which we have been exploring.

What could we include in a daily rhythm? The practices and moments you choose to include will depend on your own personality and the personalities of your children. For example some families who are much more quiet and reserved will choose to engage in more gentle and subtle ways, while some families who are more boisterous and outgoing may choose celebratory practices that are inclusive of many people, places or things. Some of these may include: Prayerful moments before meals or certain activities; nature walks noticing God's creation; mindfully aware of God's presence in mundane tasks such as washing dishes, cooking, bathing, brushing teeth; dedicating certain periods to engaged connective spacious play with our children; integrating silly play that creates laughter; offering spacious moments to hear feelings and tears; reading scripture; incorporating intentional physical touch into various activities; moments for ourselves as parents to refresh; moments where we listen and explore our own feelings and reactions to various events and triggers throughout the day; and speaking our gratitude and praise to God aloud.

There may be many more ideas you have that will suit your family dynamic and context. Below I am providing an example of a daily rhythm. You may wish to use it or to build your own. You also may wish to ease into it slowly so as not to be overwhelmed with too much change at one time.

Week-end day with young children

Morning wake-up: Snuggles, prayer of gratitude for the night's sleep and the sunrise, mindfulness of the food that nourishes our bodies (engage all your senses in the eating of it together).

Mid-morning: Connective play (10 minutes of full attention on each individual child); washing dishes (God's cleansing love); Nature walk (remember the creator, wonder about things, hold hands and use your imaginations together).

Lunch: Gather from the garden (remember the sustainer of life), gently and lovingly wash the dirt off your hands together and have a pile of scriptures on cards on the table choosing one to read.

Naps: Take time for back rubs and snuggles, prayers of needs, imaginative stories/reading together, talk about feelings throughout the morning, take this hour for personal refreshment.

Mid – afternoon: Creative activity (encourage expression of the feelings of the day or the questions you wondered about together perhaps through art or music), Dance/play silly games for laughter.

Supper: Cook together and talk about the food, where it came from and conditions in different countries; pray for various countries; express something you each are grateful for before the meal; after eating take a minute or two of silence and each listen to God's voice in your heart.

Bath time: Remember God as the wellspring of life; tenderly wash your children; play games that bring laughter with water.

Bedtime: Sit on the couch together; read a Bible story; talk about something you learned that day; have some dim candlelight and gentle essential oil smells (remind us of God's tender presence in our lives); tuck children in and pray together for their peaceful relaxation and sleep. Take this evening time for personal refreshment or working through personal healing.

Journaling Questions:

- Wherein lies the difficulty for you in creating or maintaining an ongoing rhythm? Is it difficult to create the plan, difficult to start or difficult to sustain?

- What are some concrete steps you can take to overcome the obstacles?

- How do you feel your children will respond to settling into an ongoing rhythm? What is your emotional response to this?

- What ways will each of your children respond best given their individual personalities and needs?

Applications:

- Create a plan and begin implementing.

Ongoing practices

SOULFUL PARENTING

www.ingramcontent.com/pod-product-compliance
Lightning Source LLC
Chambersburg PA
CBHW032213040426
42449CB00005B/568